Nomad Christians

Help for Fellowship-Weary Saints Lost in the Wilderness

Charles Pretlow

The Nomad Christian
Fellowship Weary Saints Lost in the Wilderness

June 2015
Copyright © Charles Pretlow

All rights reserved. Printed in the United States of America. No part of this publication may be reproduced, stored in a retrieval system, or transmitted, in any form or by any means electronic, mechanical, photocopying, recording, or otherwise, without the prior written permission of the author.

Unless otherwise indicated, all Scripture quotations are from the Holy Bible, English Standard Version ® (ESV®), copyright © 2001 by Crossway, a publishing ministry of Good Publishers. Used by permission. All rights reserved.

ISBN 978-1-943412-03-7

Published by -
Wilderness Voice Publishing
Canon City, Colorado USA
www.mcgmin.com

CONTENTS

Nomad Christians	4
These are Not Revolving Door Church Hoppers	5
Misled in the Wilderness	5
A Rush towards True Fellowship	8
Suffering from a Skewed Wilderness Faith	9
Wounded, Bitter, and Anti-Authoritarian	11
A Super-Saint's Spiritual Pride	12
Hidden Wounds and Defilements	13
Wrong Side of the Cross	14
Transformed in the Wilderness?	17
Not Trusting God for Others	19
Non-Constructive Burden Bearing	20
Carnal Spiritualism and False Voices	21
What Manner of Spirit?	22
Giving Up the Nomad-Zealot Mentality	24
What We Went Through in the Wilderness	25
Taking Courage to become Vulnerable	27
An Invisible Fragmented Remnant	28
No True Saint Left Out or Left Behind	28
A Kingdom of God People	29
About WVP Tract-Book Series	30
Contact Information	31
More About the Author	31

Nomad Christians
The Great Wilderness Exodus for the Fellowship Weary

For years, there has been a large group of devout Christians wandering in the wilderness, disenfranchised, and frustrated while in search for true fellowship. These believers wander from fellowship to fellowship in discontentment—their numbers ever increase as local fellowships everywhere slide further into the apostasy of churchianity (most fellowships are engulfed by an end-time Babylonian culture).

Totally disheartened and turned off by the backslid condition of organized Christianity, the nomad Christian gives up seeking a church home and wanders into no-man's land, finding fellowship here and there with other disillusioned wanderers.

Most do not attend church on a regular basis, receiving spiritual food from scripture and a sincere prayer life. Some find insight and encouragement from older Christian literature and obscure ministries on the Internet. While a few may find a healthy fellowship here or there but find that they have to uproot and move to attend regularly. Many visit church after church ending up attending the least corrupt as they bite their lower lip to keep from disrupting meetings in outrage over the shallow Gospel message. Moreover, most recognize the warning signs concerning America's moral downfall and approaching judgment that will include God's people.

These non-conforming believers are fed up with false national leaders and the many local leaders who go along with damning messages of an *easy road gospel*, riding waves of popularity associated with the doctrines of men and demons. (1 Timothy 4:1-5, 2 Timothy 3:1-9, 4:3-4).

These are Not Revolving Door Church Hoppers

Do not confuse these precious saints with the consumer Christian who roves continuously looking for the best deal in fellowship amenities. The church hopper is a very different breed of believer—that is to say the church hopper looks to leadership and church staff as their tireless servants who are to provide gripping, entertaining, and never ceasing performances. These revolving door believers roam from fellowship to fellowship looking for the next fad teaching, the next carnally led revival, or the next higher-level power-leader. The church hopper thrives on the continuous search for that perfect dose of spiritual Prozac that makes all their emotional and mental anguish disappear.

To the nomad Christian, the church hopper is another by-product of churchianity, adding credence to their stand against marketing the Gospel to the undiscerning and immature. However, the nomad Christian is also at great risk of deception as they strive to know Christ in the wilderness while avoiding churchianity.

Misled in the Wilderness

The nomad Christian complains of the spiritual abuse in most fellowships they visit or attend, not realizing that they themselves suffer from their own carnal motives of heart. It is easy to find fault in carnal and wayward churches, however, in the nomad Christian's mind their brand of fault finding is to them discernment and being led by the Holy Spirit.

In their seeing the faults they either take on each wayward fellowship they encounter or slide into anonymity, coming out of hiding now and again to check things out. This condition allows Satan to mislead and hinder a nomad Christian from becoming incorporated into a true last day's ministry or a fellowship that the Lord is in the process of raising up. Many a nomad Christian is blinded by the devil in recognizing a true fellowship that is under God's discipline, training, and sanctifying work.

As Satan misleads many sincere yet gullible Christians through popular false leaders and movements in these last days (as Christ warned in Matthew 24:4-5,) so too, these disconcerted wilderness Christians are highly prone to their own brand of deception.

For the *carnally* driven saint, the wilderness becomes one of the devil's better beguiling opportunities. As these dear saints wake up to the false everywhere, in their seeing they become puffed up. Indeed, they have a true call upon their lives and yearn to become prepared to work in the Lord's army and be ready on the day that God acts—however, they are stubbornly in gross denial of their own carnal motives of heart.

This condition of denial is similar to Peter's, and in this condition Satan has a right to sift as many nomad Christians as possible. The Lord attempts to build up the nomad Christian's faith in the wilderness that their faith might not fail when Satan comes to sift. (But this faith strengthening is hampered by lack of sound teachings of the work of the cross in the believer's life and recovery from wounds to the spirit and damaged emotions).

Help for Fellowship Weary Saints Lost in the Wilderness

The sifting by the devil catches them in their *pride of knowing* the truth and their cocky self-reliance, causing them to be led astray by a counterfeiting voice, often accompanied by false miracles. The initial Holy Spirit work of awakening them to the truth becomes a snare. At first, the Lord reveals and awakens them by revelation, with answered prayer, or some personal signs and wonders, or even with occasional prophetic dreams, yet when the Holy Spirit speaks to their own carnal issues, wounds, and self-reliance, they turn a deaf ear.

Insecurity, self-pity, and the need to prove their own validity drives most nomad Christians to withdraw, hide and bemoan the terrible condition of God's people. Often they have been battered and torn by other Christians who are engrossed and trapped in churchianity, or ripped by hirelings and wolves in leadership. Thus, they give up trying to minister or speak out and turn to a wilderness existence similar to a *John the Baptist* form of reclusiveness. Then, in the power of a *John the Baptist faith* personal trials eventually cause that type of carnal faith to wane and then the sifting begins, causing many to backslide and even renounce Christ.

Some do find a healthy fellowship that is in the Christlike character growing process, but their ultra-sensitivity to the carnality in others becomes a challenge to their perfectionistic and grace-less expectations. In this case most allow their own insecurities and lack of grace and understanding to stir up distrust and bitter expectations that project trouble—then the trouble does come and off they go— back into the wilderness.

I would be remiss by not offering a remedy and the Lord's ultimate goal for his wounded and disenfranchised wilderness saint. Therefore, the next portion of this message addresses how a nomad Christian can truly walk in the fullness of Christ and become part of God's end of the age work.

A Rush towards True Fellowship

In the days to come true ministries and godly fellowships will start to be recognized by nomad Christians and other dissatisfied believers, including hordes of church-hoppers. With events in the world and in this nation growing worse an exodus of the fellowship weary and consumer Christian alike will begin to take place. A multitude will begin to rush towards any kind of seemingly true leadership and true fellowship desperately looking for answers and true Holy Spirit manifestations.

The issues will be many, and true leadership will be strained in mentoring and making sincere and teachable disciples into a mature body of believers prepared to minister and live in extreme difficulties. The main challenge for the nomad Christian (and those leaving churchianity) is having a willingness to submit to the discipline of the Lord. In that discipline will be the constant directive by the Lord to embrace sound doctrine brought forth by true servant-leaders who are examples, who have learned the ropes and are walking the walk.

This will be difficult for the nomad Christian who has learned to be independent and often uncommitted to the hard work of character and relationship building amongst other Christians. God calls his people to live and work together in godly body life, where other likeminded believers learn to die to the works of the flesh. A true disciple of Christ is called to relate to others in Christ-likeness, not hide from others. Those *others*, in healthy fellowships will also be in process learning to die to carnal motives, carnal spiritualism, insecurities, jealousies, self-reliance, competition, and other thin-skinned reactions and selfish behaviors.

Any solid last day fellowship having God's hand upon it will strain towards unity in love and purity, making Christ head of all. This is the call of God today, making disciples who work together walking in the kingdom life (in the fullness of Christ)—to refresh your memory concerning this commission, read again Ephesians 4:11-16.

Suffering from a Skewed Wilderness Faith

Lack of sound instruction on Christ's teachings and New Testament principles concerning fellowship and people relationships is one of the major defects in churchianity. Indeed, most church going Christians succumb to leadership idolatry, where arrogant ministers crave the accolades of men and dare not preach how to walk in godliness. The Apostle Paul exhorts, *"Teach and urge these things. If anyone teaches a different doctrine and does not agree with the sound words of our Lord Jesus Christ and the teaching that accords with godliness, he is puffed up with conceit and understands nothing. He has an unhealthy craving for controversy and for quarrels about words, which produce envy, dissension, slander, evil suspicions, and constant friction among people who are depraved in mind and deprived of the truth, imagining that godliness is a means of gain"* (1 Timothy 6:3-5).

Likewise, the lack of knowledge and training in working out godly relationships between the members of a fellowship is also a major issue with most nomad Christians. The sacrifice of learning relationship accountability is a costly side effect for the nomad Christian when they cannot find a healthy church home. Granted, nomad Christians hide in the wilderness as a means of survival, learning to avoid the false and the corrupt that has invaded most fellowships—however, learning to work together in fellowship and dying to carnal motives is a vital necessity for maturing in Christ.

The inability to discern and ward off the wolves and game players that churchianity collects and even helps produce was a major reason the wilderness became so appealing. However, the safety of the wilderness does not allow a deepening of discerning skills or the development of spiritual strength for the end-of-the-age challenges of everyday living and ministry. (See John 17:15-19 and 1 Corinthians 5:10).

In escaping to the safety of the wilderness, the proverb, *"Iron sharpens iron, and one man sharpens another"* (Proverbs 27:17) is lost in the isolation of no man's land. In our fellowship we give this principle our own adage—that the gunk in others brings out the gunk in ourselves.

Thus, in growing up into Christ, fellowshipping with others will have relationship challenges that, if understood will help facilitate healing, recovery, and character development. It is very important to realize, *for any believer in Christ*, that relationship accountability is not to be avoided. It is God's training ground and the main arena for his discipline.

Wounded, Bitter, and Anti-Authoritarian
Renegades to any form of organized church

As mentioned, many Christians will soon be leaving false and carnal fellowships and many wilderness trekked saints will also appear at the doorsteps of solid ministries and true fellowships. With most that do come there will be great difficulties in becoming part of a healthy, growing family of God. Most nomad Christians coming will either be unable or unwilling to see, understand, and crucify their own entrenched carnal motives for serving the Lord. To them, they have learned to be content in their anti-establishment attitude and carry a self-imposed cross where an inner martyred self-righteous stance covers up their own lack of grace, truth, and Christ-like character.

Through years of seeing national leaders fall and personally experiencing failed leadership, a bitter expectation towards authority has formed. Thus, submitting to proper authority and accountability within a true fellowship will grate against their ingrained nomad ways. (That grating will not stop unless a proper understanding is reached concerning how the work of the cross in the believer's life is facilitated by God).

Years of disappointment makes it difficult for the nomad Christian to realize and sort out their own deep fears of rejection or being used and abused as they try to become part of a true fellowship. The nomad Christian will tend to be standoffish, making others feel uncomfortable, and then misread any carnal reactions in others as snootiness or cliquishness. To compensate, the nomad Christian will express their knowledge of scripture to counterbalance the insecure feelings and try to assert themselves as a spiritually more advanced Christian.

These and other issues will hinder leadership's efforts to facilitate teamwork and the development of Christlike character within the body life of a fellowship under the Lord's discipline. Unless there is a breakthrough in understanding, eventually the nomad Christian will likely recoil from embracing sound doctrine that exposes and helps crucify hidden carnal issues of the heart.

A Super-Saint's Spiritual Pride
Lacking Humility, Grace, and Truth in the Inward Being

To maintain an inner self-righteous stance the wilderness surviving believer becomes prone to project spiritual elitism that subtly elevates themselves in the eyes of others, yet they learn to deflect any praise by humble self-abasement. They appear to be on top of their sin nature and carnality by presenting an austere almost monk-like lifestyle. The Apostle Paul warned of this kind of Christian walk by stating that self-imposed mortification has "a*n appearance of wisdom in promoting rigor of devotion and self-abasement and severity to the body, but they are of no value in checking the indulgence of the flesh"* (Colossians 2:23 RSV).

Confused within by a hidden and subtle self-fulfilling endeavor to serve God, the devil slowly diverts the zealous nomad Christian from becoming a true servant-leader. Like sword packing Peter, he had zeal to fight for

Christ and clipped off the ear of one of the temple servants then later denies even knowing Christ. In similar fashion many nomad Christians pack a *trouble making attitude*. When they plunge into confronting the carnality in others, often they run and hide when the confrontation gets too hot and requires grace and truth in the Lord for healthy resolution. Learning to die to our own carnal zeal in serving Christ is very hard and requires mentoring from others who have succeeded in dying to an inner self-righteous stance and associated motives.

The hardest aspect of following Christ for most Christians, including those struggling in the wilderness is to understand and walkout Christ's covenant of grace and truth. *"For from his fullness we have all received, grace upon grace. For the law was given through Moses; grace and truth came through Jesus Christ"* (John 1:16-18 ESV) Thus, many devout believers in Christ, especially the nomad Christian will often struggle with the Old Testament laws and regulations, and the prophets—missing how these apply to us now—which should be applied only in light of the Gospel of Christ.

Few Christians today are able to work with the Holy Spirit and the written word of God in detecting hidden carnal motives that are mixed with genuine faith and obedience.

Hidden Wounds and Defilements

Neglectful, dysfunctional, or abusive parenting during childhood poses great difficulty for nomad Christians in their attempt to grasp the grace and love of God. The need to perform in order to be approved by God becomes the central drive in serving God. This drive subtly becomes a self-righteous inner stance for all of life, especially in dealing with churchianity (a term we use to describe an apostate condition where the grace of God is trampled upon and the Spirit of grace is often outraged).

This makes the Christ-like attribute of patience and grace towards themselves and others a vague or hazy concept. Legalism and perfectionism creep into their motives in serving God and interacting with others. Thus, many attempt to become a super-saint unconsciously.

As they see the waywardness in Christians everywhere they are prone to become zealots in decrying churchianity. This zeal (to point out lukewarmness and apostasy in others) increases whenever the Holy Spirit attempts to convict them of any inner issues they can't or won't see within their own hearts. Their zeal and drive for Christ and restoring righteousness to the Church actually helps cover up their own wounds and damaged emotions that sustain their own brand of carnality and denial thereof.

Wrong Side of the Cross
Suffering from a John the Baptist Faith

Many nomad Christians look to the cross as a way of life they must enact as they carnally drive a death-to-self lifestyle and at least attempt to become self-abased and holy. However, most nomad Christians are insecure and competitive and suffer from deep jealous feelings within their secret heart. Truth in the inward being and applying wisdom toward discovering the motives of the secret heart is a threat to their wellbeing. Becoming broken of their inner self-righteous stance is

Help for Fellowship Weary Saints Lost in the Wilderness

akin to literally destroying their life as a super-saint. (One of the very things the work of the cross within the believer's life is meant to do).

Perhaps the most challenging aspect of the nomad Christian's walk is overcoming their lack of understanding how to facilitate the work of the cross within the believer's life. (For that matter most believers in Christ are challenged in properly understanding how death to the carnal self-life is accomplished).

Note: A John the Baptist approach to following Christ becomes attractive for the sincere saint fed up with churchianity. This type of faith is used by Satan to blind the need to die to an Old Testament type of faith that John the Baptist lived. John the Baptist looked to the coming Christ and practiced the law faithfully, and that required a wilderness life of self-imposed hardships and extreme self-pummeling to suppress the desires of the flesh. That approach, like the prophets of old was to end when John the Baptist died as a martyr. John the Baptist dying signified the *death of the old covenant* and *a handing off* to Jesus the work of bringing and establishing the new covenant of grace, truth, and death to the old nature, and resurrection into a Christ-like nature. (See Hebrews 8:13).

"Truly, I say to you, among those born of women there has arisen no one greater than John the Baptist. <u>Yet the one who is least in the kingdom of heaven is greater than he</u>. From the days of John the Baptist until now the kingdom of heaven has suffered violence, and the violent take it by force. For all the Prophets and the Law prophesied until John, and if you are willing to accept it, he is Elijah who is to come. He who has ears to hear, let him hear." (Matthew 11:11-15 ESV).

The principle of the cross and its death to all self-driven adherence to the law brings freedom. Christ in this passage is setting forth a transition from the Old Covenant faith to the New Covenant faith, where newness of life, power over the sin nature, and freedom from flesh driven religion is found only in Christ. ***End of note.***

The commands of Christ are very poignant concerning dying to the carnal life, such as *"If anyone comes to me and does not hate his own father and mother and wife and children and brothers and sisters, yes, and even his own life, he cannot be my disciple. <u>Whoever does not bear his own cross and come after me cannot be my disciple</u>"* (Luke 14:26-27 underline added).

One cannot choose their own death-to-self processes or circumstances. When we present ourselves as a living sacrifice (see Romans 12:1-2,) we must understand and submit to what and how God brings us into various death-to-self situations. Moreover, we must recognize each event and then pick up our cross by submitting to the situation and embracing the pain of seeing our hidden selfishness and self-glorifying motives become exposed—that we might die to them.

Another saying we often share with each other is: *the flesh cannot crucify the flesh*. When we try to bring death to our inner motives by way of our own volition and ingenuity, we ultimately suppress the inner carnal desire and reprogram our outer nature to live in pious control of our life. Piously controlled living will quickly impinge upon those around us—in family life, with friends, and within the family of God in fellowship.

We short circuit Christ's work of exposing, showing, and applying his life-giving power that renews. Many Christians, especially sincere believers who are waking up to the sick condition of the body of Christ, easily fall back into carnal religious bondage—enslaved to self-imposed holiness by reprogramming themselves, only to unknowingly walk in self-righteousness. True brokenness and humility that is to be obtained in Christ's discipline is replaced by false humility and hypocrisy.

It is God's purpose to conform us to Christ. This is to be done in freedom from any religious self-effort, in his discipline and timing. *"Now the Lord is the Spirit, and where the Spirit of the Lord is, there is freedom. And we all, with unveiled face, beholding the glory of the Lord, are being transformed into the same image from one degree of glory to another. For this comes from the Lord who is the Spirit"* (2 Corinthians 3:17-18).

When we try to crucify our canal passions and desires in self-strength, we open ourselves up to the hordes of false teachings delivered by teachers who claim to know the right methods in becoming Christ-like—methods that supposedly produce successful, prosperous, and happy believers. To this, a counterfeiting spirit assists the deceived in reprogramming themselves, which ultimately preempts the transforming power of the Lord.

The following points will help us understand the more deceiving and destructive aspects of carnal driven holiness and the zealot activist approach many nomad Christians give way to. In addition, we will see God's ultimate plan in calling the nomad Christian, the lukewarm Christian, and those stuck in churchianity into true fellowship as Christ restores his bride in purity, splendor, and power.

Transformed in the Wilderness?

In Scripture, the wilderness is often used by God to hone and refine godly character within his people and especially those whom God has called to be his messengers. However, in times of apostasy and corruption within God's people and their organized religion, true believers are often attacked and forced to retreat into the wilderness for their own safety, sanity, and preservation of true faith.

Unfortunately, most true believers who give up on trying to find a suitable fellowship (there are some—but not many) find themselves on their own in no-man's land, struggling to find help with their walk and growth in Christ. Their own wounds are left undressed, where only corporate ministry by the true body of Christ in fellowship can facilitate total recovery and wholeness. The wounds of God's people everywhere are covered up and latent. Lingering past defilements, spiritual trauma, damaged emotions, and various self-centered issues are endemic—likened to Jeremiah's prognosis of his day: *"From the least to the greatest everyone is greedy for unjust gain; from prophet to priest, everyone deals falsely. They have healed the wound of my people lightly, saying, 'Peace, peace,' when there is no peace"* (Jeremiah 8:10-11).

Granted, it is better to limp along in the wilderness than to comply with the lies of churchianity that usually lead to a slow death of faith in Christ. Churchianity with its false teachings tends to groom and program believers in Christ to put their faith in man's teachings, and to live and work for the organization's agenda. The nature of false doctrine is to make believers in Christ dependent on leadership and blindly follow, not reading Scripture for themselves or learning to hear and obey the voice of Christ individually.

But without accountability with other likeminded believers and true leadership as described in Ephesians 4:11-16, nomad Christians trekking alone in the wilderness miss vital character transforming processes.

Not Trusting God for Others

Perhaps the most sorely missed aspect of being transformed into Christ-likeness for the Christian in no man's land is learning to trust God *for others*. Fears and expectations of betrayal within fellowship-relationships often obstruct the wounded or insecure nomad Christian from becoming closely involved with others. A standoffish approach to working and sharing within fellowship, even with family becomes part of the nomad Christian's carnal boundary-setting dynamic. Growing in grace and mentoring others requires getting to know others on a personal basis and being known by others with proper boundaries. Those proper boundaries are laid out in the New Testament, with the foundational guidelines of grace, truth, humility, confession, and love. Importantly, proper boundaries grow with a healthy fear of God, respect for others, and proper respect with discernment towards leadership.

The avoidance of becoming vulnerable and real in relationship to others is one of the most difficult carnal defense mechanisms any Christian must overcome. Much more for the nomad Christian, for many hide in the wilderness suffering from relationship abuses and betrayals. Like any other carnal issue this characteristic must be brought to death and the wounds supporting this personality dynamic must be healed in Christ.

Intimacy with Christ without the interference of close relationships on earth is all too easy for the nomad Christian. And for a season Christ will reveal himself to the nomad Christian while they are protected in the isolation of the wilderness. However, to be an effective disciple of Christ one must become vulnerable to the disappointments by others and not flinch when it happens.

Christ's example of holding people at a proper distance, yet being personable, open, and honest is the disciple's benchmark for Christ-like character development. Christ did not trust himself to anyone, yet he was trustworthy, approachable, non-condemning, and insightful, thus very influential in the personal lives of others.

"Now when he was in Jerusalem at the Passover feast, many believed in his name when they saw the signs which he did; but Jesus did not trust himself to them, because he knew all men and needed no one to bear witness of man; for he himself knew what was in man." (John 2:25-25).

Non-Constructive Burden Bearing

The nomad Christian does learn many aspects of true discipleship while in no man's land. However, for most, the law of Christ becomes easily misunderstood, where bearing the burden of others who struggle becomes a ministry of continual correction with little or no empathy. (See Galatians 6:1-5.) Often, when a strong, yet wounded nomad Christian does find a fellowship home, they inevitably work themselves into a position of informal leadership and gain the reputation as being the fellowship sage, giving advice and counsel, yet at the same time being aloof to the goals and plans of the fellowship leaders. They still hide in their own wilderness type fortification, unwilling to examine their own inner motives in true humility.

Pointing out the mistakes and issues in others in the guise of helping becomes their forte or gift, yet it becomes their sense of wellbeing and they begin to draw life from helping others rather than from Christ, ultimately taking the place of the Holy Spirit's work in the lives others.

Other bent character formations lurk in the wilderness for the nomad Christian where Satan brings a unique set of deception and often cultivates counterfeit gifts.

Carnal Spiritualism and False Voices
Picked up in the Wilderness

The practicing of the gifts of the Holy Spirit throughout much of Christendom has become a popular and yet a very misunderstood activity. Discernment of the counterfeit gifts is virtually non-existent, where carnal spiritualism is hoisted up as a move of the Holy Spirit in just about every sector of the body of Christ.

Carnal and false leaders push God's people towards obtaining spiritual power with little-to-no regard to the Holy Spirit's work of discipline, sanctification, training, timing, and leadership. Christians in the wilderness can also become deceived by a corrupt desire for God's power and lust after the gifts. Many nomad Christians become caught-up in coveting the power of God for reputation, or a self-aggrandized agenda, or to overcome defilements and issues of heart—just as easily as the duped Christian trapped in Charismatic-Pentecostalism forms of churchianity.

The nomad Christian becomes highly susceptible to a false shepherd's voice as they struggle alone, missing the accountability found in likeminded fellowship. Likewise, the written word of God becomes easily misunderstood and its power to become living and active is diminished without corporate discipleship interaction. Even in the wilderness, arrogance can easily take root and the deep motives of heart that are contrary to God's will and purposes remain hidden—yet seep out through carnal prayers.

What Manner of Spirit?
Some have a Zealot Mentality and Arrogant Elitism

A contrary condition of heart is a plague to most believers in Christ including nomad Christians. On the surface most committed Christians feel a true love for Jesus and are willing to follow Christ anywhere. However, when trials and relationship challenges come, the true condition of heart and spirit comes out.

As the original disciples followed Christ, on many occasions their true motives and disposition of heart became apparent, giving Christ opportunity to point out these issues. In those accounts in Scripture Christ corrected his followers and disciples and this is still the case today. Unfortunately, few discern Christ's means of correcting a carnal and contrary heart—especially when leadership is lacking Christ-like character and is aloof to the carnal conceit so many walk in. The following passage with internal footnote is an example of how

Help for Fellowship Weary Saints Lost in the Wilderness 23

easily the serious believer in Christ can develop a zealot mentality and become filled with arrogant elitism.

"When the days drew near for him to be taken up, he set his face to go to Jerusalem. And he sent messengers ahead of him, who went and entered a village of the Samaritans, to make preparations for him. But the people did not receive him, because his face was set toward Jerusalem. And when his disciples James and John saw it, they said, "Lord, do you want us to tell fire to come down from heaven and consume them?" But he turned and rebuked them. [Some manuscripts add and he said, 'You do not know what manner of spirit you are of; for the Son of Man came not to destroy people's lives but to save them.'] And they went on to another village" (Luke 9:51-56).

The nomad Christian easily succumbs to a carnal zeal to restore God's people to right relationship with Christ. This zeal often lacks humility and wisdom, where motives of heart and a spirit of destruction seeps into their prayer life causing trouble and destruction rather than intersession that is heard from on high.

The nomad Christian can easily develop a distain for anyone not aligned with their zeal, including established leadership and organized church. For the most part, this distain becomes hidden from one's own understanding and unconsciously emanates in fellowship and relationships. Thus, an aura of standoffishness and spiritual smugness often hovers over the nomad Christian like a dark cloud.

Giving Up the Nomad-Zealot Mentality
Becoming Part of the True Body of Christ

In the days to come, Christians everywhere will face increased persecution and demonic oppression. Much of this persecution has already arisen within Christianity as Christians increasingly turn against Christians. The growing schisms are led by false and carnal believers/leaders driven with anxiety and fear as they see the world falling apart. Many become radical activists with a mission to soften the Gospel, taking Christianity beyond "seeker friendly" into a "world-friendly" religion.

Already the internal meltdown has started within Christianity and soon a definite distinction between the false and the true will become glaring and confusing for the lost, the lukewarm, and the nomad Christian. The great falling away will begin and cause even greater rifts within Christianity as true ministries and fellowships begin to boldly appear proclaiming the good news of the coming kingdom. (See Matthew 24:9-14.)

For the nomad Christian, hiding in the wilderness will no longer be sanctioned by the Lord. The call to come out from amongst the false and worldly is coming to the confused church-going believer, with the urge to become unified in fellowship with true believers. The nomad Christian will not be exempt to this call of the Holy Spirit.

And with this call comes an urgent pressure to work on the heart to foster unity among the brethren and recognition of true leadership. This will require the nomad Christian to give up any vestige of the zealot approach to making things happen for God. Learning to submit to true leadership without becoming a "people-pleaser" or a "yes-boy" will be one of the nomad Christian's challenges.

There will be a great need for accountability amongst the true body of Christ, from the least to the greatest. Review Galatians and the Apostle Paul's approach to holding others accountable (including leadership) to the true Gospel. The main issue for all in the coming days will be grasping a true and solid understanding of the Gospel of Christ marked by example living.

What We Went Through in the Wilderness

These insights have been gained by way of our own wilderness journey as a ministry and for me personally, which all began some forty years ago. My personal wilderness trek started in the spring of 1975, the moment I gave God permission to do whatever it would take to change me into the person God called me to be. I concluded that prayer of commitment by asking the Lord not to stop the work, even if I asked him to stop.

Within a few months of that prayer the first of many trials and disappointments came crashing down upon my life and ministry. At the time I was a very young and naïve assistant pastor in my home town Free Methodist church, which is an evangelical holiness denomination.

I was introduced abruptly to the insidious work of a hireling senior pastor and weak conference leadership that did little to mentor, train, or exercise discernment concerning pastoral appointments. In the winter of 1975-76, I found myself looking for a new fellowship home and a different denomination to continue on in ministry. Through the following years I worked in evangelical, Pentecostal, and Charismatic fellowships until 1990 when I was led by the Lord to stop trying to *change city hall* and strike out on my own. (Stop trying to *Change city hall*, meaning that no true reform comes from within a corrupt and wayward organization, but true change comes from the outside and apart from the influence of the false.)

Nineteen ninety was the beginning of another long journey with the start of a non-denominational home fellowship where I counseled during the week and held Sunday meetings. Our support group met on Thursday evenings wherever we could use an empty church basement or someone's larger recreation room.

Through those twenty-five years we saw many Christians come and go, looking for a magic teaching or a wondrous supernatural experience to make their lack of peace and instability disappear painlessly. Case after case of heart aching accounts of abuse and roots of dark bondage were revealed and yet few embraced the work of the cross and followed Christ.

Most who did drop out did so because as a pastor I refused to do their work for them. Many wanted me, as their counselor and pastor to make their inner turmoil disappear by relieving them of the responsibility of working out their own salvation in fear and trembling. (See Philippians 2:12-18.) It was the hard work of learning and being trained in discernment to deal with the vast issues of the fallen human nature and a wounded people who passively float along, wanting to play church.

We learned quickly to avoid trying to change Christianity and not to take on battles that the Holy

Spirit was not guiding us in. We learned to work with those who God sent and grow up together and practice healthy scripturally based fellowship.

In waiting patiently upon the Lord and doing the hard work with no lime light upon us, our testing and trials proved our advancements. In this we gained much revelation and insight to develop sound doctrine that helps the sincere disciple follow Christ and not lean on us. We learned to die to our own agenda and not control and manipulate others, but present the entire Gospel of Christ with no strings attached.

And we experienced many disappointments as we learned how deceitful the human heart can become—how easily the devil can fill an evil unbelieving heart when you least expect it.

Taking Courage to become Vulnerable
Trusting God, not Ourselves or Others

To expect others not to disappoint us is something every true disciple of Christ must overcome. Trusting God for others, which includes allowing them to make mistakes and not be disappointed, is a key Christ-like character. Few seasoned believers in Christ ever achieve this godly attribute.

Instead, most walk in fear of being let down and learn to subtly control fellowship friendships, spouses, children and extended family to the extent of becoming obsessed. Many saints walk in such bondage to relationships and suffer a spectrum of relationship idolatry, from mild anxiety to extreme phobia.

Christ's discipline will take every saint (including those hiding in the wilderness) into the valley of relationship death, where trusting God for others brings freedom and peace. This work cannot be accomplished in the wilderness entirely, only by way of healthy body life within solid fellowship as guided by true leadership in Christ. We are to diligently learn to speak the truth in love and, *"to grow up in every way into him who is the head, into Christ, from whom the whole body, joined and held together by every joint with which it is equipped, when each part is working properly, makes the body grow so that it builds itself up in love"* (Ephesians 4:15-17).

An Invisible Fragmented Remnant

Unfortunately, the body of Christ is not joined and working properly together, allowing the body of Christ to grow up in divine love. Rather, what does exist is a fragmented remnant of sincere believers strewn here and there throughout America and the world. These are stuck in troubled fellowships or isolated in the wilderness, yet there are many working in true ministries and fellowships, preparing for the coming day.

This fragmented remnant has very little power and very little recognition, but presses on to the high call of God in Christ Jesus. Soon, when a threshold of fear has been reached God will call, assemble, and make visible a mighty army that knows Christ intimately. They will carry the clarion call to come out from the false and from the deceit of this world. Their message will be the good news of the coming kingdom.

No True Saint Left Out or Left Behind
True Ministries Must Be Prepared

An exodus and gathering of true believers in Christ is about to start, where the nomad Christian and sincere

Christian in fellowship alike will seek unity of fellowship with likeminded believers. The unifying catalysts for this coming final move of God will be from increased persecution, extreme wickedness, signs in the heavens, the earth reeling from one disaster after another, droughts and economic hardships, nations teetering with crime and instability, wars, Israel under continued oppression, and a very confused Christianity becoming more and more divided. The Holy Spirit will increasingly call saint after saint wherever they are to wake up, come away, and prepare.

It will be a time for true ministries, fellowships, and for unheard of servants declaring in great power the message of how to become cleansed and transformed into a true servant of Christ. True ministries and true servants who are waking up now must become prepared to handle masses of frightened people who will be desperately seeking the truth. Most importantly, each must walk in discernment, where Christian workers and leaders will need to be experts in the gifts and rightly hear Christ's voice to avoid the false and to weed out the tares planted by the evil one.

A Kingdom of God People
Love, Unity and Power for the Last Days True Church

Christ will see to it that the body of Christ, his church, will be pure, united, and walking together in love with him—in one voice. They will become a people reflecting the glory of his presence within his body—"a kingdom of God" people truly distinguished from the false and the wayward.

If you are wandering in no man's land and have given up on seeing His church become His bride, then it is our prayer that this message will warm your heart. That you would be moved to seek his face and prepare to be part of what God is about to do. To seek the Lord for direction to find likeminded fellowship.

About WVP Tract-Book Series

Wilderness Voice Publishing brings this series of short messages on sound doctrine and Christ's teachings to help the sincere Christian shed the many last day false teachings and become mature in the true Christ.

These books are designed to meet the needs of individual disciples, workers, and ministries helping each to become ready for a true and final move of God before Christ appears.

Each book focuses on a specific issue that troubles and confuses many believers today and causes harm to their relationship with Christ. Each author has worked out these very issues qualifying them to bring forth a sound teaching, rightly handling the word of truth. Wilderness Voice Publishing only publishes authors who refuse to tamper with Scripture. Many popular teachers and so-called Bible scholars take passages out of context and twist their true meaning. The following passage from the Apostle Paul's letter to the church of Corinth is our mission's banner and our charge:

"We have renounced disgraceful, underhanded ways. We refuse to practice cunning or to tamper with God's word, but by the open statement of the truth we would commend ourselves to everyone's conscience in the sight of God" (2 Corinthians 4:2)

We encourage the reader to carefully study all scripture references and seek the Lord for a clear understanding with a willingness to embrace His discipline.

To that end, may we all *"Attain to the unity of the faith and of the knowledge of God, to mature manhood, to the measure of the stature of the fullness of Christ; so that we may no longer be children, tossed to and fro and carried about by every wind of doctrine, by the cunning of men, by their craftiness in deceitful wiles"* (Ephesians 4:13, 14).

Contact Information

You can contact the author by the following:

Mail: MC Global Ministries
 Charles Pretlow
 PO Box 857
 Canon City, CO 81215
Phone: (719) 285-8542
Email: contact@mcgmin.com

Charles is available as a guest speaker. His extensive background in ministry, counseling, and end-of-this-age issues provides sound instruction on overcoming the last-days troubles and wounds to the personal spirit and damaged emotions.

More About the Author

Pastor Charles Pretlow is one of the founders of MC Global Ministries and Wilderness Voice Publishing. Charles began his ministerial work in 1974 and shares insights gained from years of study, ministry, and counseling Christians who struggled in their walk with Christ. He shares sound teachings to help equip the sincere Christian and those in leadership to effectively minister in these dark days leading to Christ's return. Charles' theology is practical, founded in years of experience and training in the discipline of the Lord.

www.ingramcontent.com/pod-product-compliance
Lightning Source LLC
Chambersburg PA
CBHW020025050426
42450CB00005B/644